NATIONAL GEOGRAPHIC

THE LAND AROUND US

Deserts

MARY TULL

PICTURE CREDITS
Cover, pages 9 (border), 11 (border), 13 (border), 15 (border), 17 (border), 19 (border), 21 (border), 23 (border), 25 (border), 27 (border), 29 (border), 30–31 (background) Photowood Inc./Corbis; page 1 Jim Erickson/Corbis; pages 2–3 Pete Saloutos/Panoramic Images/National Geographic Image Collection; pages 4–5 (background), 9 (left) Brian A. Vikander/Corbis; pages 4, 17 (left) Charles and Josette Lenars/Corbis; pages 6–7 (background) Medford Taylor/National Geographic Image Collection; pages 8, 25 Thomas J. Abercrombie/National Geographic Image Collection; page 9 (top right) Maria Stenzel/National Geographic Image Collection; page 9 (bottom right) Kevin Schafer/Corbis; page 10 Annie Griffiths Belt/National Geographic Image Collection; page 11 W. Wayne Lockwood, M.D./Corbis; pages 12, 13 (right) Michael and Patricia Fogden/Corbis; page 13 (top left) Nigel J. Dennis, Gallo Images/Corbis; page 13 (middle left) Craig Aurness/Corbis; page 13 (bottom left) Jonathan Blair/Corbis; page 14 Tiziana and Gianni Baldizzone/Corbis; page 15 Michael S. Lewis/Corbis; page 16 Pierre Colombel/Corbis; page 17 (right) Wolfgang Kaehler/Corbis; page 18 Melisa Farlow/National Geographic Image Collection; page 19 Nicole Duplaix/National Geographic Image Collection; page 20 Reza/Webistan/Corbis; page 21 Maynard Owen/National Geographic Image Collection; page 22 Charles O'Rear/Corbis; page 23 Garry Adams/Index Stock Imagery; page 24 Stone/Getty Images; pages 26, 27 (left) Richard Nowitz/National Geographic Image Collection; page 27 (right) Steve Kaufman/Corbis; page 28 Royalty-Free/Corbis; page 29 (left) Tony Robers/Corbis; page 29 (right) Buddy Mays/Corbis; page 32 (background) Owen Franken/Corbis; page 32 (bottom) Nevada Wier/Corbis.

Produced through the worldwide resources of the National Geographic Society, John M. Fahey, Jr., President and Chief Executive Officer; Gilbert M. Grosvenor, Chairman of the Board; Nina D. Hoffman, Executive Vice President and President, Books and Education Publishing Group.

PREPARED BY NATIONAL GEOGRAPHIC SCHOOL PUBLISHING
Ericka Markman, Senior Vice President and President, Children's Books and Education Publishing Group; Steve Mico, Vice President, Editorial Director; Marianne Hiland, Executive Editor; Anita Schwartz, Project Editor; Jim Hiscott, Design Manager; Kristin Hanneman, Illustrations Manager; Diana Bourdrez, Picture Editor; Matt Wascavage, Manager of Publishing Services; Sean Philpotts, Production Manager.

MANUFACTURING AND QUALITY MANAGEMENT
Christopher A. Liedel, Chief Financial Officer; Phillip L. Schlosser, Director; Clifton M. Brown, Manager.

ART DIRECTION
Dan Banks, Project Design Company

BOOK DEVELOPMENT
Nieman Inc.

CONSULTANTS/REVIEWERS
Dr. Margit E. McGuire, School of Education, Seattle University, Seattle, Washington
James F. Marran, Social Studies Chair, Emeritus, New Trier Township High School, Winnetka, Illinois

BOOK DESIGN
Steven Curtis Design, Inc.

MAP DEVELOPMENT AND PRODUCTION
Dave Stevenson

DIAGRAM DEVELOPMENT AND PRODUCTION
Steven Wagner

Published by the National Geographic Society
Washington, D.C. 20036-4688

Product No. 4J41759

ISBN-13: 978-0-7922-4565-0
ISBN-10: 0-7922-4565-2

Printed in The United States of America

18
10 9 8 7

Cover: Sand dunes in the Sahara
Page 1: Moroccan girls
Page 2: Monument Valley Tribal Park, AZ

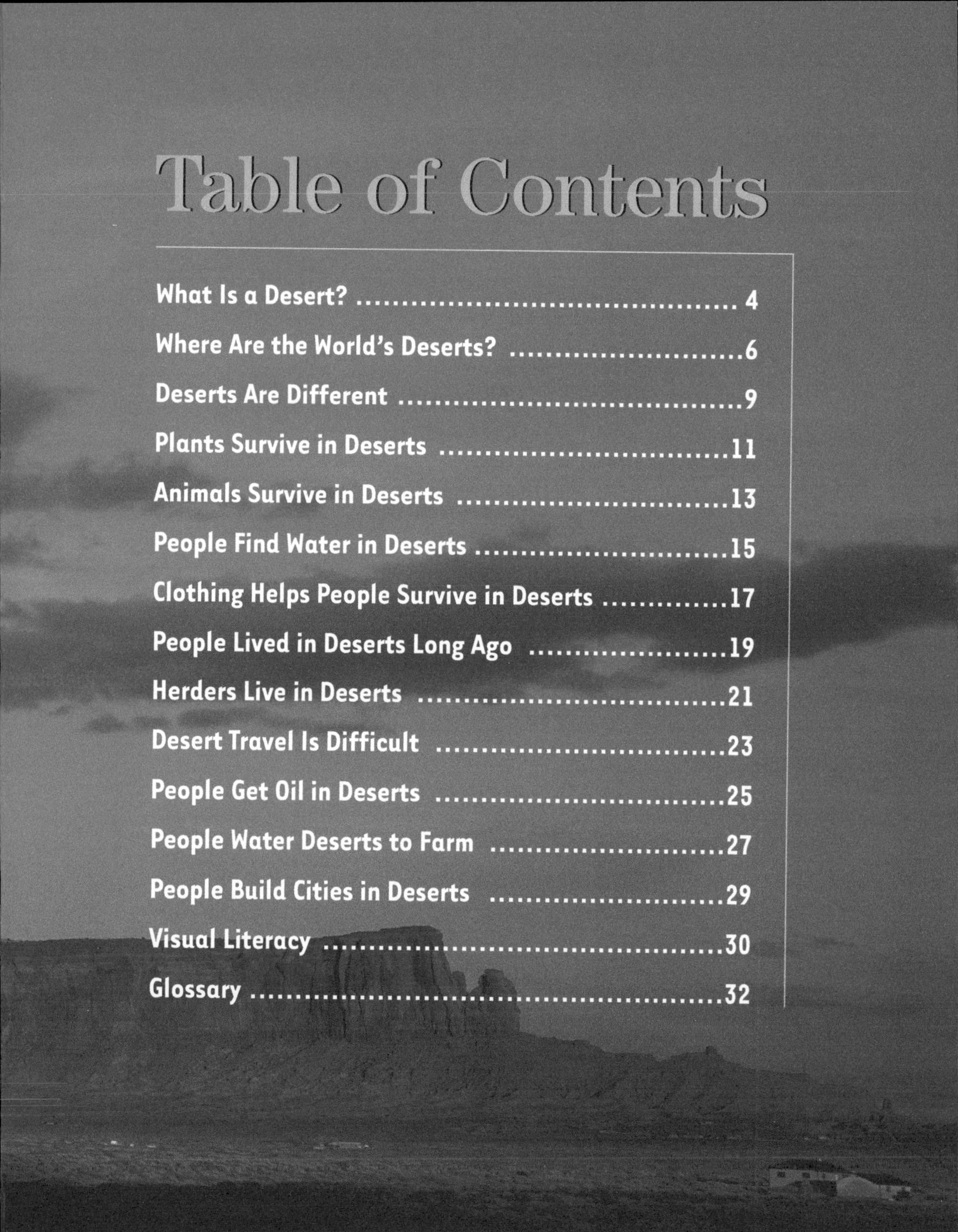

Table of Contents

What Is a Desert?

The driest places on Earth are **deserts**. They get 10 inches (25 centimeters) of rain or less a year.

Some deserts are covered with sand, but others are rocky. Strong winds blow across sandy deserts and form dunes, or sand hills.

Deserts are the hottest places on Earth, but not all deserts are hot. Some are very cold. Even in hot deserts, the nights can be very cold. One thing is sure. Everything about deserts is extreme! Desert winds churn up sandstorms that last for days. When it rains in a desert, it pours! Instant rivers flood the land. Then, just as fast, they dry up and disappear. They leave dry **riverbeds**.

Because of these extreme conditions, deserts are difficult places to live in. Yet, animals and people can find water. A desert place with water is called an **oasis** (oh–AY–sis). There living things can survive.

Sandstorm
Oasis
Dunes
Sandy Desert
Dry Riverbed

Where Are the World's Deserts?

Earth has many deserts. The **continents**, Earth's seven largest bodies of land, are Africa, Antarctica, Asia, Australia, Europe, North America, and South America. All the continents have deserts.

The hottest deserts can be found in two wide bands of land on either side of the **Equator**. The Equator is an imaginary line around the middle of the Earth. The coldest deserts are found in the parts of Earth that are farthest north and farthest south.

The Sahara is the world's largest desert. It is so big that it stretches across the continent of Africa. Is the Sahara a hot desert or a cold desert?

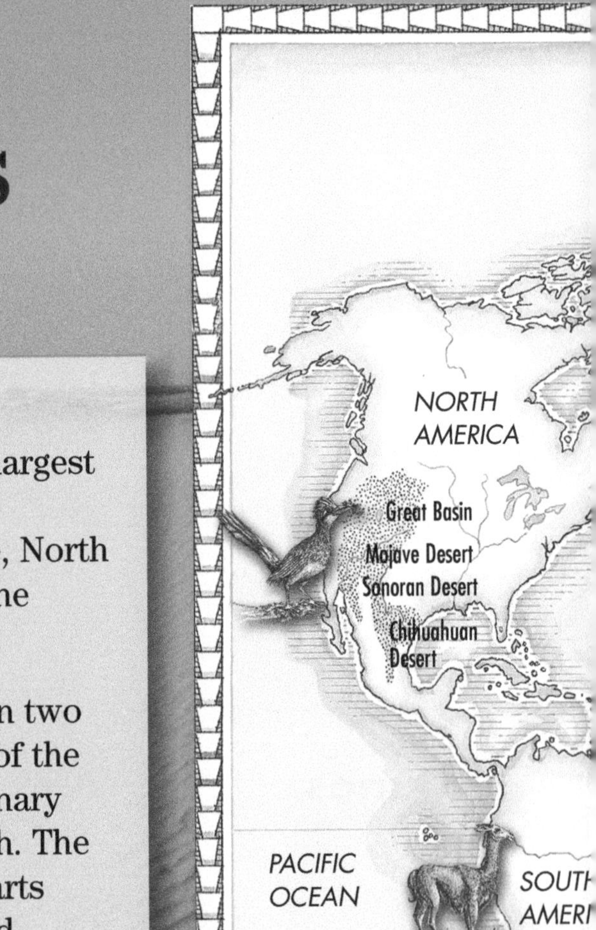

ASIA
EUROPE
Gobi
Kara Kum Desert
Taklamakan Desert
PACIFIC OCEAN
ATLANTIC OCEAN
Iranian Desert
Thar Desert
Sahara
Arabian Desert
AFRICA
EQUATOR
INDIAN OCEAN
Namib Desert
AUSTRALIA
Kalahari Desert
Australian Desert
N
W
E
S
0 500 1000 1500 miles
500 1000 1500 kilometers
ANTARCTICA

Deserts can be hot or cold.

Camels crossing the Sahara,
the world's largest hot desert

Deserts Are Different

Frost patterns in a desert in Antarctica

Deserts are very different from one another. Hot deserts can have temperatures above 100 degrees Fahrenheit (38 degrees Celsius). Yet, the frozen land of Antarctica is a desert too. Temperatures there are way below freezing. Remember, it is dryness that makes a desert.

Mountains in a cold Arctic desert

Most deserts are flat, but some have mountains. Sandy deserts can have dunes as tall as buildings. The sand dunes change shape when the wind blows. In other deserts, the land is stony and stays the same all the time.

There are also high deserts and low deserts. High deserts are found on land high above **sea level**, the level of the ocean surface. There the land is cold most of the year. Low deserts are near sea level or below it. They are hot.

Desert sand dunes in the American Southwest

Desert plants trap and store water.

Saguaro and organ pipe cacti

Plants Survive in Deserts

Desert plants have special ways of going long periods without water. The cactus plants of North America have wax-coated stems that hold water. Their spiky thorns keep thirsty animals from nibbling their stems and stealing their water. Many desert plants have roots that travel wide and deep to collect underground water.

A creosote bush

The saguaro (suh–WAHR–oh) cactus can grow more than 50 feet (15 meters) tall and live to be more than 150 years old. It stores water in the center of its stems and roots.

Leaves help desert plants survive. Some leaves have short hairs to trap water. The leaves of the creosote (KREE–uh–soht) bush have a tough, oily skin to keep water inside. Desert holly bushes have light-colored leaves. They reflect sunlight away from the plant to help it stay cool.

Desert animals live in a harsh world.

Kangaroo rat

Animals Survive in Deserts

A grasshopper's tough shell helps it survive.

A camel's eyelashes, lips, and nostrils protect it from blowing sand.

A chuckwalla hides from the sun in a desert cave.

Deserts are home to many animals able to live in dry conditions. Some, such as the kangaroo rat and the African gerbil, can get water from the seeds they eat.

Animals have other ways to protect themselves from harsh desert conditions. Camels have long eyelashes to shield their eyes from blowing sand. They can also close their nostrils to keep out sand. Desert insects have tough shells and waxy wings to protect them.

Many desert creatures don't come out in the hot sun. They come out at night, when it's cool, to find food and water. They stay in homes underground during the day. Some desert snakes and toads sleep during the very dry spells. Some bury themselves in the ground until it rains.

Sidewinder, or horned rattlesnake

In deserts, water means life.

Tuareg at an oasis

People Find Water in Deserts

In desert villages, people dig wells. Water lies in rocks and in lakes or rivers deep below the surface. Wells tap into this **groundwater**.

Sometimes, an underground river comes to the surface. The water spreads out on the ground and makes an oasis. An oasis is a beautiful place. Trees grow and offer shade from the hot sun. Birds and animals come to drink the cool water.

Herders and camels in the Sahara

The Tuareg (TWAH–reg) people of the Sahara live in tents. They follow their herds as the animals search for food and water. Tuaregs often travel many miles to reach an oasis and get water. They let their animals drink. Then, the Tuaregs fill the skin bags they use to carry water and move on.

Clothes guard against sun and sand.

This Tuareg woman's clothing and tent shield her from the desert sun.

Clothing Helps People Survive in Deserts

Clothes are not just to make you look good. Clothes give protection. In deserts, people wear clothing that shields them from heat and cold and blowing sand.

A sandstorm blows over a Tuareg village.

Many people who live in deserts wear long, loose robes. These protect their skin from the hot rays of the sun. These robes may be white to reflect, or throw back, the sun's heat. The clothes worn by people in the desert are of dark colors too. For example, the Tuaregs are known for the dark blue color of their robes.

A Tuareg's head covering protects him from blowing sand.

The robes are made of heavy, tightly woven cloth. They protect a person from stinging, windblown sand. In the desert, people often cover their heads with cloths. These special head coverings keep sand out of their eyes and mouths.

Deserts were homes to ancient peoples.

Visitors explore the ruins of an Anasazi cliff house.

People Lived in Deserts Long Ago

Deserts have been home to humans for about two million years. In Australia, early people painted pictures on the walls of desert caves. Their paintings show how they lived and what they believed. Some paintings show the animals they hunted. Other paintings tell their religious stories.

The Anasazi (ah-nuh-SAH-zee) people lived in the deserts of the American Southwest long ago. They built their houses on steep cliff walls there. The Anasazi understood the plants and animals of the desert. They ate grasshoppers, roots, and the sharp, prickly buds of the yucca tree. They knew which plants showed where to find water underground. They dug ditches to catch the little rain that fell each year. Then, they used it to water their fields of beans and corn.

Desert people of Australia painted pictures on rocks.

Herding is a desert way of life.

Nomadic herders in Afghanistan

Herders Live in Deserts

Herding is raising animals such as sheep or goats. It is a way of life for many people who live in deserts. Herders eat the meat from their animals. They use their animals' milk to make yogurt, cheese, and butter. Herders use animal hides, or skins, to make clothing, saddles, and tools. In many desert lands, animals are more important than money.

Some herders are **nomads**, moving from place to place. They carry tents and follow their animals as they search for food and water. In Afghanistan, nomadic herders raise goats and sheep. Goats do well in the desert. They aren't picky eaters. They eat almost anything, even clothing!

The Afghan nomads make tents from goat hair. They use sheep wool to make blankets and beautiful rugs. At night, they sing songs and tell stories about their lives as desert herders.

Desert roads are steep and rocky.

Llamas marked with ribbons showing who owns them

Desert Travel Is Difficult

Deserts are usually rough country. Most are large, empty stretches of rock or sand. They have few good roads or towns. Some deserts have mountains too. They are not easy places to travel through.

In South America, the Atacama Desert stretches from the Pacific Ocean right up the steep sides of the Andes Mountains. The people there use **llamas** to help them travel. Llamas are related to camels, but are much smaller and have no hump.

Mountain roads in the Atacama Desert are steep. They are narrow and covered with rocks. The llamas don't slip. They know how to walk on rocky paths.

The people of the Atacama Desert tie different colored ribbons to the ears of their llamas. That way they know who owns each one. People use their llamas to carry food and supplies in packs woven from the animals' own wool.

A woman of the Atacama Desert

Oil is an important resource.

An oil pipeline in Saudi Arabia

People Get Oil in Deserts

Petroleum (puh-TROH-lee-uhm) lies deep below Earth's surface. Petroleum was formed hundreds of millions of years ago from the remains of ocean plants and animals. When it is pumped to the surface, it becomes oil.

Workers drilling for oil

The modern world runs on oil. Oil provides fuel for cars, trucks, trains, ships, and airplanes. Some power plants burn oil to produce electricity. Thousands of products are made from oil.

Much of the world's oil comes from the Arabian Desert. The Ghawar oil field of Saudi Arabia is the largest in the world. Oil workers use drills to dig deep into the ground. After the oil reaches the surface, it travels through pipelines. Then, ships carry the oil to plants where it is **refined**, or cleaned. Once oil has been refined, it is used to make everything from footballs to floor wax.

Desert farmers grow many crops.

An Israeli farmer in his field of crops

People Water Deserts to Farm

It takes lots of water to grow fruits, vegetables, and grains. A desert is usually not a good place to farm. Yet, people have ways of watering the desert to raise crops.

An irrigated onion field in Israel

In Israel's Negev Desert, farmers **irrigate** the land for farming. To irrigate means to bring water to dry land. Often, people use pipes or dig ditches. The Negev is a part of the Arabian Desert. Its ground is hard and cracked. Farmers bring water from 90 miles (145 kilometers) away. The water travels through pipes. When it reaches the orchards and farms, special tubes release one drop of water at a time at the base of each plant. Plants and trees get just the right amount of water to grow. Not a single drop is wasted. Now, fruit trees bloom in the desert. Rows of corn, onions, and cucumbers grow under the hot desert sun.

Cities strain desert resources.

Phoenix, Arizona

People Build Cities in Deserts

A fountain at a Phoenix resort

The city of Phoenix, Arizona, is in the desert. Like many other desert communities, Phoenix puts stress on its **environment**, or natural surroundings. More than a million people live there. They like the warm climate and sunny weather. The water for Phoenix comes through the desert from the Colorado River. It gives the city green parks and water fountains. People build swimming pools. Phoenix uses a lot of water.

Phoenix also uses a lot of electric power. Homes and buildings are air-conditioned.

A golf course in Phoenix

More people come to Phoenix every year. City traffic creates air pollution. Phoenix's power plants burn coal and oil that also pollute the air. Because Phoenix uses a lot of water, the people, plants, and animals in nearby places get less. As Phoenix and other desert cities grow, problems such as these get worse.

Visual Literacy

Circle Graphs about Deserts

The information in some of the books you read may be shown in circle graphs. A circle graph shows the parts that go together to make up all of something. Because a circle graph looks like a pie cut into slices, it is also called a pie graph. Use the circle graph below as you go through the following steps.

How to Read a Circle Graph

- **Read the title.** The title of a circle graph tells you the subject, or what the whole circle shows.
- **Read the labels.** The circle graph's labels tell you what each part shows.
- **Connect the information presented.** Compare the different parts of the circle graph.

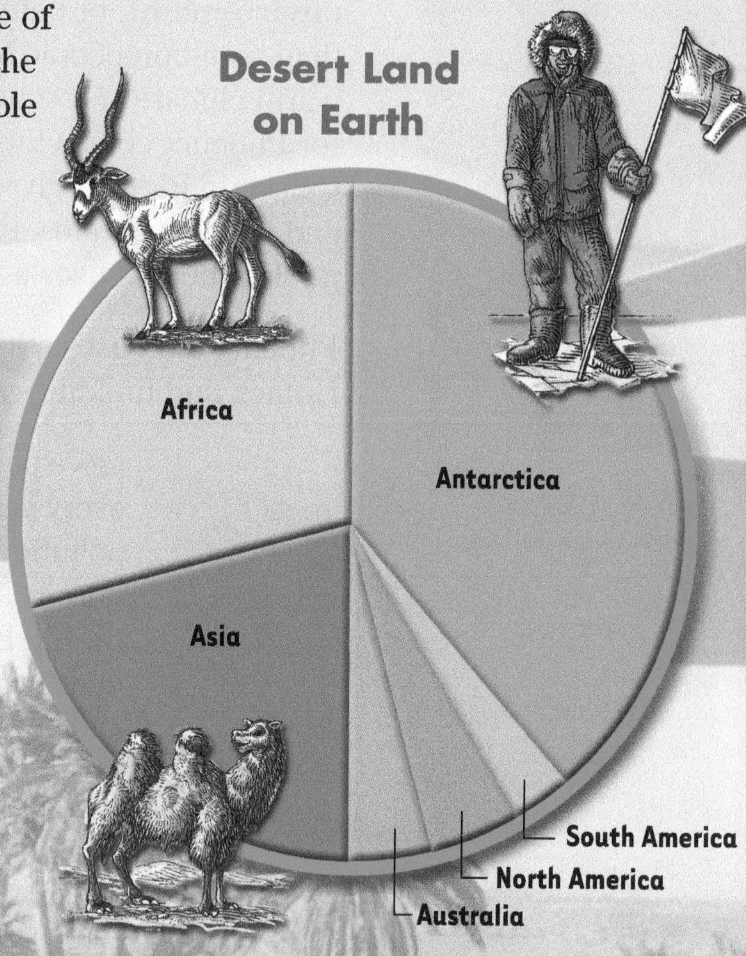

Here's another circle graph. What does the whole circle show? What does each part of the circle show?

Deserts of Australia

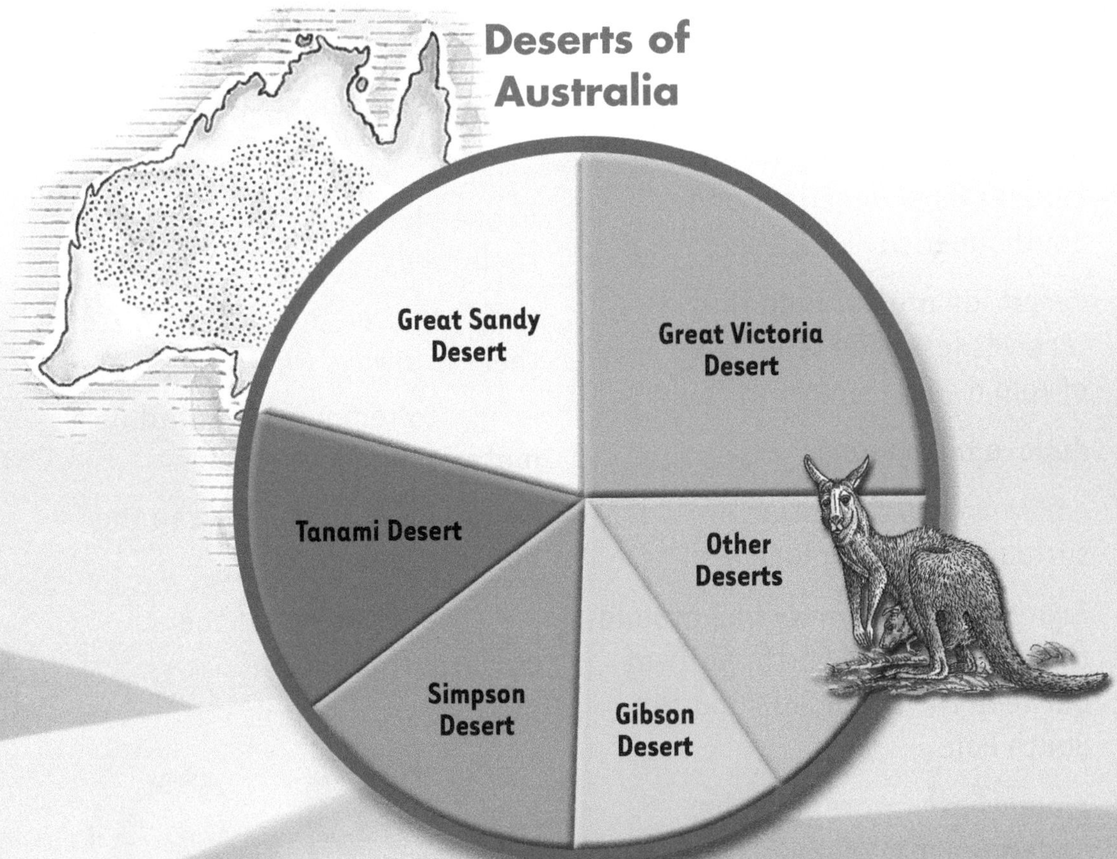

Thinking about the Circle Graphs

- Use the graph on page 30 to answer the following questions: Which continent has the largest amount of Earth's desert land? Do Africa and Asia combined have more or less desert land than Antarctica?
- Use the graph above to answer the following questions: Is the Great Victoria Desert larger or smaller than the Gibson Desert? If you combine the Great Sandy, Simpson, and Gibson deserts, is the result larger or smaller than the Great Victoria Desert?

Glossary

continent one of Earth's seven largest bodies of land—Africa, Antarctica, Asia, Australia, Europe, North America, and South America

desert an area of land that receives less than ten inches of rain a year

dune a hill of sand

environment the natural surroundings of a place

Equator an imaginary line around the middle of the Earth, halfway between the North Pole and the South Pole

groundwater water that lies underground

herding raising animals for meat, milk, hides, and other products

irrigate to bring water to dry land, often by using pipes or digging ditches

llama a South American animal related to the camel

nomads people who do not live in one place but move with their herds

oasis an area in a desert where there is always water

refine to remove unwanted material and make pure

riverbed the area between the banks of a river

sea level the level of the ocean surface

A woman and her child in a desert in Central Asia